This Catechetical Prayer Book
Was Presented to

O LORD,
TEACH ME TO PRAY

A CATECHETICAL PRAYER BOOK
FOR PERSONAL USE

Richard F. Bansemer

Illustrated by
Vickie DeVilbiss

The American Lutheran Publicity Bureau

CONTENTS

To teachers who imitate Christ
and to their students
who will learn to teach

"What would it help me if Christ was born a hundred times . . . if nobody told me that it happened for me."

Martin Luther, W.A. 15,783 25/12/1524

"The most momentous duty of one generation to another is its education."

David Bittle, first president of Roanoke College, Salem, Virginia

INTRODUCTION

This book takes the teachings of *The Small Catechism* before God in prayer. It is for use by students, pastors, and parents, and anyone else who wishes to grow in "the fear and the knowledge of God." It is one thing to know the contents of the catechism. It is quite another to ask God for guidance and wisdom through its teachings.

Praying "correctly" involves both honesty with God, and concern for the things that God has raised as significant for us. This little prayer book is designed around the basics of the spiritual life, as it's lived in human form.

These prayers lean heavily upon Martin Luther's explanation to the basics of the Christian faith as found in *The Large Catechism.*

Special appreciation is extended to Vickie DeVilbiss of Annapolis, Maryland, artist, who created the six drawings for this book, to Ray E. Blanset who provided interpretive text for the drawings, and to Frederick J. Schumacher, Connie Seddon, and Dorothy Zelenko of the American Lutheran Publicity Bureau who made the publication of this book a reality.

I AM

"I AM" is the name by which God made himself known to Moses in the burning bush at Horeb and called Moses to deliver the people of Israel from bondage in Egypt (Exodus 3).

After the miraculous events of the Exodus, God made a covenant with his people in the words of the Ten Commandments, the epitome of our duties toward God and one another (Exodus 20).

The burning bush with the words "I AM" in the trunk, superimposed on the stone tablets of commandments, reminds us that God who has delivered us, calls us to covenant life expressed in the Ten Commandments.

I AM

I. THE TEN COMMANDMENTS

Part 1: Commandments directed toward God

The First Commandment
"You shall have no other gods."

What does this mean for us?
Answer: We are to fear, love, and trust
God above anything else.

Prayer 1

Lord God, I come to you with words, understanding that you will listen to me so closely, that even
if I don't say everything right, you will know my
heart, and read my mind, and answer my prayer.
People who know you better than I say that you are
much more willing to listen than we are willing to
pray. Thank you for being so big, that even my littlest
prayer is important to you.

You tell me, God, that you want to be more
important in my life than everything else put together.
You tell me I cannot have any other gods, just you. I
don't think I worship any other gods, although there
are many things I like a lot. I think I'd like to know

you better, to make sure those other things don't become as important to me as you are.

You tell me that I should respect you above all else, even before I know you very well, which is hard to do, since I have so much to learn of your love for me. You tell me that I should trust you with my life. Help me learn what it means to have confidence in you, total confidence, for my own good.

Finally, God, you tell me I should love you. Already I've learned that you love me, but now you tell me that you want love from me too. I am so glad to try to do this. Sometimes I feel like no one wants my love, but you do. Help me remember this every time I am sad or feel so alone. Help me love you, just like you love me. Amen.

Prayer 2

Heavenly Father, how can I ever trust you like I should? I am not able to let loose of everything, believing that you will take care of all. I keep wanting to take control of my life, seek for happiness, and have my share of good things. I am being told that trusting in you is more important than all the things I want that I think will bring me joy. Even if I accept that teaching in my mind, I don't know how to do it in my life … how to let go, how to trust you completely, how to believe you will guide my way every day. What am I to do when things go wrong? What am I to do if you ask more of me than I am ready or able to give?

Lord God, though I know I have a lot of growing to do in the faith, please help me listen to your Word, your promises to care, and your record of faithfulness with those who suffered because of faith in you. Help me have confidence in you and your promises, because I'm already beginning to see how empty and disappointing life can be if I am the center of it all. Amen.

Prayer 3

Lord God, how am I to love you if I am afraid of you? Your commandments feel rigid, and I am not able to keep them all. I know that your laws are good, because they show me my sin, and let me know what you expect from me; but Lord, I am sometimes afraid that you will punish me for doing wrong. You know I do wrong over and over again. How can I not be afraid of you? I keep breaking your commandments. Will you punish me harshly?

I have been taught that it is impossible to love you unless faith accepts your forgiveness. My faith is so weak and my sins are so big, but I do want you to be my God, my one and only God. I do not want to live every day with guilt. Help my faith grow stronger every day by practice—by believing in your forgiveness of me.

Lord, if I forgive somebody else the wrong they do to me, I know it is very hard not to hold it against them, even when they're sorry for what they've done. So forgive me, if I put my weakness up against your strength to forgive. Forgive me if I worry about punishment, when what you want to give me is forgiveness. You are God, and you can forgive so much better than I can. You forgive and forget, at once and forever. Help me take comfort in your daily forgiveness, knowing that when you forgive, you really do forgive, and when I accept it, it is a clear sign that I am being faithful to you. Amen.

The Second Commandment
"You shall not take the name of the Lord your God in vain."

What does this mean for us?
Answer: We are to fear and love God so that we do not use his name superstitiously, or use it to curse, swear, lie, or deceive, but call on him in prayer, praise, and thanksgiving.

Prayer 1

Lord God, all your names are holy, but every day I hear people misuse them, as though your names were nothing special. I know you must not like people using your name lightly, but I've been taught that you are especially angry when we use your name in a way that isn't truthful. Because you are "the truth," you do not want me using your name to pretend the truth when I am lying. You do not want my lips saying what my heart knows is wrong.

I've been taught, Lord, that you don't want me to pretend to be your person, when I really don't want to be your follower. You don't want me making believe to others that I have a greater faith in you than I really do, or that you've told me things you haven't told me. There are many false people who do this, and you don't want me to be one of them. You just want me to be your loyal follower. Lord, thank you for not making me have to pretend. Thank you for letting me grow in the faith, and not be a super saint all at once. Thank you for not making me live a lie by false holiness. It is enough for you that I honor your name, by putting all my confidence in you. Amen.

Prayer 2

When things don't go my way, Lord, and I think you could have made a difference, sometimes I blame you. Although you never want me to turn away from you for any reason, sometimes it feels to me like I don't trust you with my whole heart. Maybe it's because I'm hurt that you didn't do what I wanted you to do, or something didn't happen for me that I wish would have happened, so I take it out on you. Lord, when I do this, I know I am not honoring your name, your Godliness, your ability to always know what is best for me and those I love. I know, when I feel this way, that I have a long way to go in the faith, but I am glad that I am already your person, even if not perfectly so. You know what I am made of, and you don't let my moods and feelings interrupt or lessen your love for me. Thank you, Lord, for being that big about it … bigger than I can be, which is why you are God, and I am not.

In the days and months and years yet to come for me, help me be more like you, by letting no misunderstanding or disappointment lessen my love for you. Amen.

Prayer 3

Lord God, how pleased you are when I use your name the right way. You are happy to have me call you by name for any need that I might have. You are happy to hear me talk about you by name to friends and neighbors. You don't even mind me using your name if I am called upon by government to tell the truth when it is necessary and required.

Lord, when trouble is near, remind me to call on you. In any moment of need, when I ask for help from you, I honor your name. When I am faithful to what you teach, I am honoring your holy name.

Even as you know me by name, may I use yours with love and devotion, now and forever. Amen.

The Third Commandment
"Remember the Sabbath day, to keep it holy."

What does this mean for us?
Answer: We are to fear and love God so that we do not neglect his Word and the preaching of it, but regard it as holy and gladly hear and learn it.

Prayer 1

Lord God, Sundays are such wonderful days for play, that using that day to gather for worship and Sunday School seems to intrude on my fun. I understand that years ago people needed to be freed from hard labor for a day a week, for the sake of resting their bodies and minds. Now, Lord, I'm like most others I know. I like to use my "off time" for myself, for leisure, even for adventure. Going to church sometimes gets in my way.

Lord, you tell me to keep this day special, to set it apart for both of us, that we may grow closer together. You tell me that I need this day more than you need it. You tell me that I need to be seen out in public as your person, and that I need to see others growing in their faith too. You tell me that we people need each other's Sunday witness, else the faith is something just private between the two of us. You insist on being more than my private God. You want me to be proud of you and your way, and to let the whole world know that I believe.

Help me, Lord, to keep the special day holy, by hearing your Word read and preached in church with others. Help me understand that I need others, if I am to learn what it means to be part of your movement on earth, your strong kingdom coming within the weak kingdoms of this world. Amen.

Prayer 2

Lord God, sometimes I overestimate my strength. I think I can do more than I really can, or I think that

I am not as tired as others notice that I am. Sometimes I think I don't need a day of rest, a sabbath day, a Sunday spent with you. Life can be so interesting that I don't want to miss out on any of its fun and joy, yet you tell me that I need to step back, regularly, to see what's going on in my life. You want me to think as well as act, to notice as well as to respond, to ask questions of myself, as well as to enjoy myself. You give Sundays, and other days like them, to do these things. You give Sundays so that we may know who else there is who reflects and sings, who learns and prays, and most of all, gives thanks to you for all your goodness.

Lord, I know I don't thank you often enough. Although I know that you are behind every good and wonderful event in my life, and this very moment of conversation with you is a holy gift of love from you, I am so easily distracted from the time it takes, that my mind wants to wander away from you. I am not able to list all that I know that you do for me every day, much less the countless other things that you do for me that I do not know about. Nevertheless, I thank you, inadequately of course, but I thank you.

Help me keep this commandment, Lord, every day, and not just on Sundays. Help me make you such a regular part of my daily life, that all my days with you on your earth are sacred. Amen.

Prayer 3

Lord God, your Word is what makes any day holy, any thing holy, anyone holy. I know I need your Word more than any other words, for whenever you speak, it is a holy matter. You use your Word to keep Satan out of my life, to show me your path, and to provide for all goodness upon the earth. Without your Word, no day could exist. With it, all days are holy.

Lord, create in me such a yearning for your Word, that I look for opportunity to hear it preached and taught. Keep me from letting worship become mere entertainment or habit, for in so doing, I abuse your Word and derive no benefit from it. Help me listen to your Word as though you are speaking personally to me about your will in my life and in this world. Tune my ear to your voice so precisely, that my life may be lived like a piano worthy of a master's touch.

Lord, I am so glad that I know whom to thank. Thank you for this day, this holy time, and your constant care. Amen.

Part 2: Commandments related to our neighbors

The Fourth Commandment
"Honor your father and your mother."

What does this mean for us?
Answer: We are to fear and love God so that we do not despise or anger our parents and others in authority, but respect, obey, love, and serve them.

For Sons and Daughters

Prayer 1

Lord God, how strange that you expect me to honor my parents, and not just love them. You have lifted up these unique people in my life and have directed me to give them the highest honor possible. Above all others, you tell me that you distinguish father and mother, and place them next to yourself in deserving respect.

Lord, you know as I do, that no one has perfect parents, yet your command still stands. You are not asking me to agree with them on everything, but you are telling me to treat them as persons with whom you've entrusted a great responsibility and blessing. You have given them to me, and though they sometimes fail to understand me, or I fail to understand them, you tell me to revere them as persons given a mission from you for me.

Thank you, Lord, for my parents. Though we have had our difficulties with one another, do not let me deprive them of the respect they are due, for in giving them honor, I am thanking you for their love of me. As we grow in years together, give me the will to care for them, even as they have cared for me. Amen.

Prayer 2

Lord, thank you for my parents, my guardians, and for all those who care about me and point to you as my true Creator and Sustainer. Do not let me ever forget or take for granted their loving work on my behalf. Remind me, that when I am able to honor them rightly, it is your Holy Spirit that makes this possible. Let me never forget all that they have done for me. If it be your will, give me the opportunity to do it for others in the years that are yet to come.

Lord, in the promise you've attached to this commandment, "that we may have long life in the land where you dwell," may I see your purpose for loving my parents. It is not only for them, but also for me, that this commandment is given. You want me to honor my parents for the sake of happiness … theirs, mine, and yours. It is good to know that I can make all of us happy by loving your way. Thank you, Lord, for your guidance. Amen.

For Parents

Prayer 3

Lord, you have given me, as a parent, a big responsibility. You have given me holy work to do, because it is work you've privileged me to do. It is not always easy to love my child, yet you tell me to do so.

My adult friends, Lord, have situations almost impossible to imagine. Some are parents all by themselves and have no help in the raising of their children. Some parents don't love their children, and treat them badly. Others have reached out in special love and have adopted children, just like you have adopted me in Holy Baptism, making me your child. Surely, they are very special parents. Still others give temporary care for children who are victims of tragedy. Lord, help us all to do your will with those you've placed in our care.

Thank you, Lord, for every child. Give me the patience to teach them your way, the wisdom to answer their questions, the love to reflect your way, and the understanding to know how precious each child is in your heart. For letting me be your arms, thank you. For letting me be your voice, thank you. For letting me let love happen between us, thank you, Heavenly Father, thank you. Amen.

Prayer 4

Lord God, you have lifted up very high the work of parents. It is so high, that none of us can do it without a constant measure of help from you. You make our parenting holy, because you have made us your personal representative. You let us bring children up in the faith. Next to worship of you, Lord, you have given us the highest work there is to do.

Some parents and guardians have no regard for you, and think that faith is so much silliness. They bring no honor to our task. Help us to help them become worthy of respect, by loving you and their children as gifts from you.

Remind me, Lord, to give honor to my own parents too. Though I did not always understand them, I do not know, either, all that they endured on my behalf. Thank you for my work as parent. Thank you for my parents. May the devil be angered by my appreciation, for he has tried often enough to frustrate our love for each other. Amen.

For Those Facing Divorce

Prayer 5

Lord God, how deep the pain is for those of us who suffer from divorce. It is so impossible to understand, so fearful for all.

If it's my parents experiencing it, I wonder how they'll manage without each other, and I wonder how and where I'll fit in their lives. I worry if maybe I could have changed things, even though that isn't so. I wonder if they'll be okay, and if I'll be okay.

If it's me experiencing it, I have many of the same worries. We are all facing unknown futures. We all feel very alone.

Heavenly Father, Beloved Son, your family was broken too … broken by death, broken by separation, broken by the sin of this world. Help me keep all of us in my prayers, because we are, now and always, full members of your family, the family of God. Amen.

The Fifth Commandment
"You shall not kill."

What does this mean for us?
Answer: We are to fear and love God so that we do not hurt our neighbor in any way, but help him in all his physical needs.

Prayer 1

Lord God, all my prayers with your commandments until now have been about you and me, or my parents and me, but now you make me think about my neighbor. Now you place me in community beyond immediate family, and give me Godly guidance for living.

This commandment about killing seems easy to keep, until Jesus' explanation from the Sermon on the Mount is added. Yes, I do get angry with others, and they with me. Yes, I have called others names, and I have insulted those I don't like, just like they have done to me. That all of this behavior is a form of killing is hard for me to accept. It doesn't seem quite that bad. I would not murder someone, Lord. I know I shouldn't do these other things either, but they don't seem so bad, unless, of course, it is being done to me by them.

Lord, I must admit that I have been deeply hurt by people I thought would never let me down. I have died a little, when it's happened—-I have felt that something precious was taken away from me, something that was once alive and good is gone. Help me remember this before I do it to another. *Even if they deserve it*, keep me from doing it!

Lord, you won't let me off the hook. You expect me to be good to my neighbor, because you are good to me. You expect me not to follow bad examples by returning name calling for name calling, anger for anger, misery for misery. I will need a lot of help from you, Lord, to do this. Amen.

Prayer 2

Lord, revenge is automatically in my heart, I know. You tell me that I must not harm another for the bad they do to me, even if they deserve it. You tell me this, because I think you already know, that revenge does not bring peace, just more bitterness.

Lord, how can anyone keep this commandment? It is too hard. You expect us to be calm and gentle toward our enemies who give us grief, taunt us with harsh words, and harm us. You are asking me to be very different from the people of the world. You are showing me a way to be different that seems most impossible to accomplish. Lord, I don't want to be a doormat.

Lord, teach me to calm my anger, to learn patience and to have a character so strong, that I don't have to be passive, like a doormat, but I can be active, like your Son, Jesus, who knew how to handle enemies. Help me learn of the ways he took care of critics and enemies without sinning; how he learned how to be angry, but without sin. Amen.

Prayer 3

Lord, in this commandment, as you call upon me to do good for my neighbor, I admit that I am too often a reluctant neighbor. You want me to help in times of need and to protect as I am able, but I seldom notice what's going on next door, much less what's happening around the world.

If I could, Lord, I would call only the person next

door my neighbor. You teach, though, that I must *be* neighborly to all. In this big world, you have made all human beings my sisters and brothers. What am I to do if it does not matter to you what continent I live on? All humans are your children. Each of us is the apple of your eye. Each is my brother or sister.

How differently you make me see my sisters, Lord, when they are abused by anyone in any land. How differently you make me see the hungry, when they are my blood relatives. How differently you make me see my brothers, when they live lives without feelings. How differently you make me see anyone who is slave to a machine, in bondage to business, in prison, or merely lonely. Because of you, they are my kin.

In this commandment, Lord, you have given me a great family. Spare me from myself that I may find joy in meeting my relatives of every race and every land. Amen.

The Sixth Commandment
"You shall not commit adultery."

What does this mean for us?
Answer: We are to fear and love God so that in matters of sex our words and conduct are pure and honorable, and husband and wife love and respect each other.

For the Young Single Person

Prayer 1

Lord God, how intimately you are involved with me. You have made me a little lower than your angels, and far above your animals. You care about the way I share myself sexually with another, for you made me in your image, and you have said about all of your creation that "it is good."

Not only do you know my deepest longings, Lord, but you also know my deepest needs. Keep me from wrongly using what you've given me for pure joy and sharing. Help me use the gift of sex rightly, that I may one day completely share myself with another, and another person with me, according to your will and purpose.

Lord, it is difficult to follow your commands in a world that ignores you. I don't like being different from my peers. I don't want them to think there is something "wrong" with me. How am I to satisfy my own curiosity about the other sex and still keep your commandment? I ask you for patience and self-control to wait for marriage before accepting the delights of being in full partnership with another person.

If, Lord, I fail to keep this commandment, I know that you will not despise me, but I also know that you will be saddened if I don't believe in the value of your way. Help me learn faithfulness now, by being obedient to your command. Amen.

For the Married

Prayer 2

Lord God, you have placed us all upon earth through the miracle of conception, requiring that male and female unite with one another in the creation process. You will let no one of us be so self-sufficient that not needing another is good, or even a matter of choice. Clearly you have said it, that it is not good to be alone. Thank you for establishing the family. Thank you for establishing the holy estate of matrimony.

I ask for your help to share myself intimately with my spouse in ways that are good. I know your commandments are a gift for my sake. You want me to enjoy this life fully, but not selfishly. You have provided delightful ways for me and my spouse to share ourselves completely with each other. May we marvel over your gifts and find continued delight in one another.

Keep me faithful to my spouse, Lord God, all the days of our wedded life together, and let no temptation to either of us win away our heart from the other. I ask for your strength to love rightly, for my own sake, and for my spouse's. Amen.

For All

Prayer 3

Lord God, out of love, you forbid adultery, because you care immensely about my neighbor, and you know how my wrong actions affect relationships in other people's lives forever. What a strange twist you put on adultery. It's so easy to suppose that all you want to do through commandments is keep good order, deny too much pleasure, and make life legalistic, but you really are looking out for others when you tell us what is best for us.

Lord, since I am somebody else's neighbor, I hope that they will keep your commandment too. When we take our eyes off of you, we all hurt one another so easily. It happens without thinking, without seeing all the people involved in adultery, not just the two of us.

It's not only my body, Lord, that you command me to keep pure. You expect me to guard my lips from shameful words and keep my heart open to your grace. Without your grace, Lord, my best intentions will fail. I know it all too well. So, be my God, and visit me in the worst times of my life, as well as when I am on my best behavior. Know me through and through, but do not desert me, even when I deserve it. Be present, Lord, with grace and understanding, for this world is too big and too confusing to handle alone. Amen.

The Seventh Commandment
"You shall not steal."

What does this mean for us?
Answer: We are to fear and love God so that we do not take our neighbor's money or property, or get them in any dishonest way, but help him to improve and protect his property and means of making a living.

Prayer 1

Lord God, you know how dear "things" become to me. I'm just like everyone else. We all like our stuff, and we are ready to have more and more of it. We take great joy both in receiving gifts from others, and in giving things to people we like. We like to earn and shop, get more and accumulate. You know, don't you, that our things are sometimes too precious to us?

Lord, when I can't afford to get what I want, help me wait until time and work make the purchase possible. Keep me from dreaming up evil ways to get what I desire. Better yet, Lord, keep me from wanting too much, unnecessary things, for no "thing" brings happiness for long. Remind me how little I use the things that were so important to me just a couple of years ago. Remind me that stuff, sometimes good, can sometimes be bad for me too.

Above all, Lord, keep me from getting anything dishonestly. I don't want to be a thief by any definition. And help me help my neighbors keep what is theirs, that we may all respect each other and each other's property. Amen.

Prayer 2

Lord, there are so many ways to steal, that most of it isn't even named "theft." Rich people do it to poor people, making them poorer. Poor people do it too, out of desperation, I suppose. Even people who don't work an honest hour for a wage are stealing. And the overpaid likewise steal. How am I to avoid all these possibilities, knowing full well that there are thousands of other ways to steal too?

Lord, keep my needs simple and my motives pure. Let me be vigilant within, that no "easy money" tempts me to take it. If I gain a great sum, but lose my self respect and incur your anger, I have become a poor, poor loser.

When I become a victim, Lord, of someone's dishonesty toward me, sometimes I feel right in being just as thoughtless to another myself. Remind me of your word and my pain, so that I will not inflict revenge upon any one else, even if opportunity comes to get even with the one who wronged me. Somewhere, Lord, this nonsense of vengeance and greed has got to stop. Let it stop with me, for my own sake, for my neighbor's sake, and for your own world's sake. Amen.

> **The Eighth Commandment**
> "You shall not bear false witness against
> your neighbor."
>
> **What does this mean for us?**
> Answer: We are to fear and love God so
> that we do not betray, slander, or lie
> about our neighbor, but defend him,
> speak well of him, and explain his
> actions in the kindest way.

Prayer 1

God, I've known what it's like to be talked about
by others and have to defend myself. It makes me feel
angry. Either I didn't do or say what was reported, or
what happened wasn't anyone else's business … at
least not public business. Help me remember how
much gossip upset me, so that I will not do the same
to my neighbor.

It doesn't matter, does it, Lord, whether the "news"
is true of false. You don't want me spreading bad
things about my neighbor for any reason, unless I am
willing to take the matter to the authorities. You don't
want me demeaning another. You don't want me to
make anyone look bad, for when I do, it reflects more
on my character than on theirs.

How dangerous is my tongue, Lord. It does me in
whenever I am not on guard. Keep me from speaking

lies, and from spreading gossip, even if it is true, for it does no good to my neighbor whom you love like me. Amen.

Prayer 2

Lord God, I can't pretend not to know something negative about another. Sometimes I wish I didn't know what's been told me. What should I do with those who tell me bad things?

Lord, I'm sorry for encouraging others by my nosy curiosity. I want to learn how to want to hear good things about my neighbor, instead of bad. I know I cannot expect good things to be said about me, if I say bad things about another.

In these private words to you Lord, I raise up my weakness before you regarding lies and gossip. Make me more careful when talking about my friends and neighbors. Good reputations are so precious, and so fragile, Lord, that I ask you to help me keep a good one for myself, and help my neighbor to do the same. They are so very hard to restore when damaged. Keep me from stealing my neighbor's good name. Give me the courage to defend others when I see them under attack. Help me do this in obedience to your command, and out of a growing love for my neighbor. Amen.

The Ninth and Tenth Commandments
"You shall not covet your neighbor's house."

What does this mean for us?
Answer: We are to fear and love God so that we do not desire to get our neighbor's possessions by scheming, or by pretending to have a right to them, but always help him keep what is his.

"You shall not covet your neighbor's wife, or his manservant, or his maidservant, or his cattle, or anything that is your neighbor's."

What does this mean for us?
Answer: We are to fear and love God so that we do not tempt or coax away from our neighbor his wife or his workers, but encourage them to remain loyal.

Prayer 1

Lord God, I like to think that these two commandments are easier ones to keep, but I know better. Even as I have seen others envy me when I had something special, or was with someone special, I also know how to be jealous. It is so hard to be content with who I am and what I have. Since I was very little I've been taught to gain and get ahead, to succeed and take a full measure of the world's pleasures. Now I hear you warning me to be careful that I do not seek any supposed happiness at the expense of my brother, my sister, or my neighbor.

Lord, I have envied other people their friends and wished they were mine instead. I have watched good things happen to not so good people, and I wonder why they are so fortunate. I often wish that I were as rich and prosperous as others who seem to be able to go anywhere, do anything, and buy anything that suits them. I know that this is coveting, and it does me no good.

As your person, Lord, teach me to seek contentment not from things, but with you. You have given me friends. Thank you. You have given me food, shelter, and clothing. Thank you. You are looking out for me. Thank you. Amen.

Conclusion

What does God say of all these commandments?
Answer: He says, "I the Lord your God am a jealous God, visiting the iniquity of the fathers upon the children to the third and the fourth generation of those who hate me, but showing steadfast love to thousands of those who love me and keep my commandments."

What does this mean for us?
Answer: God warns that he will punish
all who break these commandments.
Therefore we are to fear his wrath and
not disobey him. But he promises grace
and every blessing to all who keep these
commandments. Therefore we are to
love and trust him, and gladly do what he
commands.

Prayer 1

Lord God, how good your commandments are!
What could have been merely laws to restrict me, are
guides to direct me. What could have been seen as
burdens, you've shown to be wise. Though I spend all
my days trying to keep your word, I know that I shall
not succeed entirely, yet I am so grateful to you for
your abundant love. You will not let me go, even when
I fail.

Throughout all these commandments, Lord, I see
you telling me to put you first in all my living. You
are God, even when I don't want you to be. You alone
are God, even when I try to make something else
godly. You want to be the delight of my soul *and* my
body. You want me to have joy, and you know that
joy will escape me forever if I look for it in the wrong

places. You tell me to look for you, and when you are near, I will also find joy.

Thank you, God, both for warning me of danger, and attracting me to your way. Let me live as though your commandments are not trifles to take or leave as suits me, but your will, your holy will, your special way for me to live with my neighbors and with you. You are a kind and loving God.

May these words become more important for me to keep than all other laws placed upon me as a citizen of town or country. You are my God, and I want none other besides you. Make this true, Lord, now and forever. Amen.

CREATED, REDEEMED, CALLED

The drawing expresses the content of the three articles of the creed.

The lines across the world suggest the breath or word of God, which calls all creation into being.

The crown of thorns and butterfly remind us that Jesus Christ redeemed us with "his holy and precious blood" and gives us new and eternal life because "he is risen from the dead and lives and reigns to all eternity."

The Spirit of God is symbolized by the dove. God's Spirit calls us through the gospel to believe, to know, to pray, to live a new life as a people of God.

CREATED. REDEEMED, CALLED

II.   THE APOSTLES' CREED

The First Article
"I believe in God, the Father almighty, Maker of heaven and earth."

What does this mean?
Answer: I believe that God has created me and all that exists. He has given me and still preserves my body and soul with all their powers. He provides me with food and clothing, home and family, daily work, and all I need from day to day. God also protects me in time of danger and guards me from every evil. All this he does out of fatherly and divine goodness and mercy, though I do not deserve it. Therefore I surely ought to thank and praise, serve and obey him. This is most certainly true.

Prayer 1

Heavenly Father, how good it is to know whom to thank for all I am and all I have. Before I knew my name, or yours, you took care of all my needs. You

are so great. What you do for me you do for all
the people on the earth, even those who don't
know your name or care about you in any way.
For all of us you have made the wind to blow and
carry the seed, the sea to move with tides pulled
by the moon, the sun to shine to lighten the day and
make plants grow, and the distant stars to flicker,
as a constant reminder that you are so much bigger
than my mind will ever imagine. Heavenly
Father, how sweet your name. You are unlike the
fathers of this world who are loving. Because you
are Heavenly, you love perfectly. You are unlike the
fathers of this world who desert and let down. You are
Heavenly, forever faithful, always providing the daily
necessities and pleasures of your people.

I am your creature, Heavenly Father. I am your
beloved child. Nothing I have done makes this so. You
make it so. Thank you, Heavenly Father. Amen.

Prayer 2

Heavenly Father, no one else could do what you
have done … and continue to do all day every day! You
create the world and keep it going, never missing a beat.
You tend this earth like one big garden, providing
enough food for all your people, if we could but learn
how to share it.

Father, sometimes bad things happen in nature,
and people want to see it as an "act of God." It bothers
me to think of innocent victims of storm and disaster,
and makes me wonder why you didn't keep the calamity
away. Many people use thoughts like these to fix the

blame on you. They say you could have stopped the tragedy, but you didn't. Sometimes they even say you made it happen.

Help me understand the difference between your power to create and keep life going, and earth's own mechanism for physical life. I must learn the difference between loving you, the Creator, and the creation. It is you, alone, who are worthy of worship. Amen.

The Second Article

"I believe in Jesus Christ, his only Son, our Lord. He was conceived by the power of the Holy Spirit and born of the Virgin Mary. He suffered under Pontius Pilate, was crucified, died, and was buried. He descended into hell. (Or, He descended to the dead.) On the third day he rose again. He ascended into heaven, and is seated at the right hand of the Father. He will come again to judge the living and the dead."

What does this mean?

Answer: I believe that Jesus Christ—true God, Son of the Father from eternity, and true man, born of the Virgin Mary—is my Lord.

At great cost he has saved and redeemed me, a lost and condemned person. He has freed me from sin, death, and the power of the devil—not with silver or gold, but with his holy and precious blood and his innocent suffering and death. All this he has done that I may be his own, live under him in his kingdom, and serve him in everlasting righteousness, innocence, and blessedness, just as he is risen from the dead and lives and rules eternally. This is most certainly true.

Prayer 1

Lord Jesus Christ, true God, how good to know God by knowing you. How good it is for you to have a name like mine, a name I can call at any time, for any reason. How good to know what God would be like if he were only a human being. Thank you for being both human and divine, at one and the same time. Thank you for knowing what it's like to be us, and for showing us what it's like to be Godly. Amen.

Prayer 2

Lord Jesus, part of my problem is thinking that I don't need a redeemer. Sometimes I feel pretty good about myself, and sometimes I feel pretty rotten, but overall, Lord, I don't want to think about needing a "Savior." If I *need* a Savior, that means I cannot save myself. That means I need outside help. That means I can't clean myself up good enough to be your perfect son or daughter. How humiliating.

Lord, you won't let me save myself will you? You know it is beyond my power. You won't let anyone do it, because no one else has the power, just you. No saint is saintly unless you say so. No one on earth is good enough for heaven, unless you forgive completely. How am I to have any self-esteem, if you tell me that I do not have within me the spark of my own salvation?

Lord, "self-esteem" has become a god among us, and you keep moving me away from that concern. You keep telling me that it's not just me you love, but brothers and sisters in the world I don't even know. You keep making salvation much bigger than the saving of just me. You keep moving me into relationships with other people, like me, whom you have touched with love through your death and resurrection.

Lord Jesus, I don't want to live without you, and I know that you don't want to live without me either. What's more, you don't want the two of us living as though there's no one else who has come under the influence of your love. You put me among a multitude of believers. You put me in a faith family for support.

Lord Jesus, you go so far beyond self-esteem that my selfish concern seems trite. You live among us, now and forever. There can be no higher esteem, self or otherwise, than this. Thank you for being my God. Amen.

Prayer 3

Lord Jesus, I know that who you are and who I am makes it impossible for our relationship to be on an equal basis. Though you call me "friend" and are always beside me, I am not your equal, nor is anyone else. You are so much more than my buddy. You are God, and I am not. You are the Creator, and I am your creature. You are the redeemer who raises from the dead, and you make all people, not just me, the singular object of your love. You won't let me have you all to myself. You keep pushing me into the company of your living saints, gathered as your church.

Help me learn all that you've done to make my salvation possible. Help me understand not only why it was necessary, but more importantly, how much you had your eye on all of us, not just me, when you did it. Help me want to see all the faithful as dearly as you see them. Help me see them as my family of faith, regardless of gender or race, country or continent. When I see them, Lord, in need or in worship or at work, you say that I am seeing you too.

Lord, let someone see you in me too. Amen.

The Third Article

"I believe in the Holy Spirit, the holy catholic church, the communion of saints, the forgiveness of sins, the resurrection of the body, and the life everlasting. Amen."

What does this mean?

Answer: I believe that I cannot by my own understanding or effort believe in Jesus Christ my Lord, or come to him. But the Holy Spirit has called me through the Gospel, enlightened me with his gifts, and sanctified and kept me in true faith. In the same way he calls, gathers, enlightens, and sanctifies the whole Christian church on earth, and keeps it united with Jesus Christ in the one true faith. In this Christian church day after day he fully forgives my sins and the sins of all believers. On the last day he will raise me and all the dead and give me and all believers in Christ eternal life. This is most certainly true.

Prayer 1

Lord God, Holy Spirit, it is most difficult to call you by this name. My generation has all kinds of "spirits," but none of them are called "holy." We usually suppose that "spirit" is an impulse, or a mood, or a force. We get in "the spirit of things," or have "school spirit." We don't think about you when we think about spirit. It is more of an attitude than a being. Some people even think it is a spark within, something that is born within us, but none of this is about you … just about us.

Lord Spirit, you are not an emotion, but God. You are not a feeling, but presence. You are not an urge to let go, but a hunger for knowledge. You make me want to know God. You make me want to grow in the faith, though all the world counsels me to leave you alone. You haunt me like a ghost, forever reminding me of what's missing in my life. You keep drawing me away from myself and my needs, to others and their needs. No wonder you are not very popular.

Lord God, Holy Spirit, do not give up on me. Do not let me be so content that you become invisible in my life. Do not let me grow deaf to your word. Do not let me grow callous to the pain of others. If this happens, if I turn my back and harden my heart against my neighbor, I know I have lost your Holy Spirit. Keep calling me, shouting at me, pulling me back, showing me your need in others. I need to know you more than myself. I ask you, Holy Spirit, to shout louder, or softer, whichever it takes to make me listen. Amen.

Prayer 2

It is such a big word, dear Spirit: "Sanctification." It smacks of haughtiness. It sounds too religious to be real. It would not make much sense to my friends.

Yet, dear Spirit, you call me to grow in the faith. That's all there is to it. Just grow. Keep on keeping on, and do not give up on God, because you don't give up on me. Just look out for your work in my own life, the life of others, and in the world. That's all there is to it. Acknowledge that you are here and busy. Admit it. That's what you say. Look *and* see. Listen *and* hear. Taste *and* savor. Feel *and* be touched. Smell and know the essence of good gifts from you, gifts of food, field, forest.

Lord God, Holy Spirit, you are so easy to explain away. The world thinks it is gathering the harvest, but no one knows the mystery of a seed. The world thinks it's in charge, but you make the earth revolve and the seasons come. The world thinks it's very smart, but no one will ever find you in a test tube or a laboratory. You are beyond us all, mixing the chemicals you've created, according to your own design, and infiltrating physical life with the spiritual. No one knows how you do this, Lord. No one knows, but you do.

Keep me humble, Lord Spirit, so that I may be open to worlds unknown, to thoughts beyond the limits of my own reason, and to your influence. Amen.

Prayer 3

Lord God, Holy Spirit, believing in you is letting myself grow in faith. I know I cannot win heaven from you, even if I were to become as holy as Abraham or Mary. No one can be holy alone. You do it. You give it, instead. I know I don't have to grow in faith for my salvation's sake, and I am glad for that, else I would surely perish. I've given up such nonsense already, but Lord, Spirit of God, I do want to grow in the faith with you. It's not just for me that this is important. It's a thank-you to you and a gift for my neighbor. That is all.

Lord Spirit, thank you for the gift of forgiveness among my fellow believers. We need each other so much more than what we want to admit. We would bypass one another, except that you keep insisting that we deal with one another by facing our successes, our failings, and our sins. You make us want our neighbor to succeed as well as ourselves. You show us the joy of our neighbor's salvation, as well as our own. You put in our minds the joy of resurrection, not only for ourselves, as individuals, but also for our friends in the faith. Lord Spirit, I did not figure out the faith on my own. I had to be told. You sent a host of people ahead of me, who have made it possible for me to learn the faith from them. You give no one of us the privilege of figuring you out alone. You use us, Lord, now and forever, for blessing each other. Amen.

ABIDE IN ME

"I am the vine, you are the branches … if you abide in me, and my words abide in you, ask whatever you will, and it shall be done for you."

These words express a living relationship with God as well as the essence of prayer rooted in the will and kingdom promises of God.

God's hands are always open to those who abide in him, seeking to know his will.

ABIDE IN ME

III.   THE LORD'S PRAYER

The Introduction
"Our Father, who art in heaven."

What does this mean?
Answer: Here God encourages us to believe that he is truly our Father and we are his children. We therefore are to pray to him with complete confidence just as children speak to their loving father.

Prayer 1

Heavenly Father, you tell me to pray. You give me no choice but to do it, if I would be your person. You tell me to be in touch with you every day. You want me to do this because whenever I pray, I admit that you are superior to me, and that I need your grace and help. Lord, it is humbling for me to think I have needs that I cannot manage by myself. Everyone tells me to pick myself up and to put my own life in order. You keep saying that I cannot do that without you. You keep reminding me that as a creature, I need you, the Creator, else all my efforts at self-improvement are futile and senseless. You will not let me get my life arranged without you, unless I want to live without you, which I do not want to do.

Heavenly Father, I pray to you for help beyond my own understanding of "help." I think I am praying for daily assistance in coping and making decisions, but you know I need much more than this. You know my needs for companionship, for you nearby, for your voice and your presence and your Holy Spirit, else my life that looks full will be empty and lonely. Keep giving me what I really need, dear Father, and not just what I ask for, and as time passes, open my eyes to see all that you are doing. Amen.

Prayer 2

Lord God, Heavenly Father, I've been taught that my prayer is just as holy as a saint's. I've been taught that you yearn to hear from me, every day, just like you did the disciples, and that my prayer is precious to you. I know I have need for prayer, but it is so easy to forget to do it. At night I am sleepy, and in the morning I'm always in a hurry to get my day going. Help me to pray the prayer that Luther teaches: "I come to you, dear Father, and pray, not of my own energy or because I am worthy, but because you tell me to be in touch with you, and you promise to listen and answer."

So much do you want me to pray, you even give me the words to use in the Lord's Prayer. Though I write and pray a thousand prayers a day, none is better than the one your Son teaches me. Help me to remember him teaching me, even as I talk to you with the special words he gave us to know you better. Amen.

The First Petition
"Hallowed be thy name."

What does this mean?
Answer: God's name certainly is holy in itself, but we ask in this prayer that we may keep it holy.

Prayer 1

Our Father, my Father, how hard it is for some to call you by that name, yet Jesus even called you "Abba," "Daddy." You are the Father of us all, and you do fathering rightly. You don't make the mistakes of earthly parents. You are heavenly, beyond the limitations of earthlings. Because of this, your chosen name for yourself is precious and holy.

Father, your special name for yourself is hardly ever taken in vain. Your Son's name is taken in vain all the time, as is "God," but "Father" isn't. You have made it nearly impossible for us to corrupt your good name by choosing "Father" for yourself. We may not think very much of many of the fathers of this world, yet your name is still holy.

Father, God, if I use any name for you wrongly, I

know I am not hallowing this special name for you either, so help me to use all names for you rightly. Let me never use your name to tell a lie, for that is dishonoring you, which is worse than dishonoring myself.

How good, Lord God, Heavenly Father, to know how you want to be known. How good to have a daddy that is good, beyond doubt; good, beyond imagination. Amen.

Prayer 2

Father, if I do not call upon you, I do not hallow your name. If I do not hallow your name, I do not know who God is. Help me come to you as you are, as you have revealed yourself to us, as you continue every single moment to be both creator and protector.

Father, mothers and fathers on earth get tired of parenting. You never seem to weary of being there for me, ready to guide or discipline, loving or warning me of your displeasure. When I am open to both sides of your love, the embracing and the chastening, I hallow your name the best. Help me, then, to hear you as you are, always knowing that you are on my side and know what's best for me and others.

Lord Father, even if I don't keep your name holy, as I should, it is holy anyway. You are so holy, that, in the end, you cannot be spoiled by me. I can spoil who you are for others, and I can ruin my side of our relationship, but you are still holy, still my Father. Help me remember, therefore, to name you proudly. Amen.

The Second Petition
"Thy kingdom come."

What does this mean?
Answer: God's kingdom comes indeed
without our praying for it, but we ask in
this prayer that it may come also to us.

Prayer 1

Heavenly Father, your kingdom came when you
sent your Son Jesus to live among us, and to deliver
us from the powers of evil. Your kingdom came with
Jesus, who brings us life and salvation, and battles for
us against the enemies we cannot handle by ourselves:
sin, death, and the devil. Your kingdom came with
Jesus, and he is still among us, doing your work for
us. You must love us greatly to send us your Son. You
must love us greatly, if you were willing to have your
one and only Son die for our salvation. What a king
you are. What a kingdom he brings.

Lord Father, you tell us that your kingdom can be
real to us *now*, if we receive it by faith. We don't have
to wait for the hereafter. Help us to put ourselves in
those places where we can hear your Word, so our
faith may increase, and the certainty of your kingdom
may be ours.

Our Father, I pray for myself individually too.

Help me work to overthrow that other kingdom, that entices me with pleasure, promises me happiness, but is based on lies. Help me dare to believe that sin, death and the devil will all be overthrown by you, when your kingdom comes in its fullness; when your Son returns in power. Amen.

Prayer 2

Lord Father, Luther teaches that you offer us beggars "great and princely gifts." Sometimes we foolishly ask only for "a dish of beggar's soup" or a crust of bread. We mock your offerings when we do not accept your priceless gift of presence. We mock you when we settle for something less than the banquet you set before us as your beloved people.

Father, everyone else in my life tells me to ask for less, and to be satisfied with a little. You tell me to ask for more, to seek you like a great pearl, to look for you in every event of my life. You tell me to see you present at every meal, no matter how meager it is, and to see you there as partner in my life. If you are with me, Lord, your kingdom has come, your kingdom is here already!

Father, it is not just the food of this world that you offer as evidence of your presence. You promise that which is eternal, can never spoil, can never fade in the brightest of light. Your son, Jesus, is that light, and he is coming back. Your kingdom comes again, for good, and forever. Give me the faith to look with expectation and excitement for that glorious moment. Amen.

> **The Third Petition**
> "Thy will be done on earth as it is in heaven."
>
> **What does this mean?**
> Answer: The good and gracious will of God is surely done without our prayer, but we ask in this prayer that it may be done also among us.

Prayer 1

Heavenly Father, the more I try to honor your name and see your kingdom already here, the harder it is to do what you would have me do. I keep wanting to do things my way, and you keep reminding me to do things your way. It's as though your will and my will are in constant battle with each other. It's as though I am personally under attack whenever my will is under attack. It feels like you want to take complete control of my will, and if you do, you will be in control of me.

I don't know why I am so afraid of this. Getting my way usually turns out badly, and you know what's better for me than I do myself. I am so afraid of letting you have your way with me. Lord Father, is it the devil that stirs me up against you? Does he want my will as strongly as you want my will? He uses all the world to lure me away from you. He shows me all the pleasures and fun of forgetting you, but as soon as I do, I make myself miserable and miss you. "Thy will be done," dear Father, not mine. Take my will, my life, and let me see what you can do with a person like me. Let me see you work with clay this poor. Let me be made into someone new, for your sake, and my own. Amen.

Prayer 2

Father God, there is a war going on inside of me. Two forces are out to win me over—you and the enemy. The enemy is your enemy and mine, and he seems to be winning much of the time. His allies are powerful. He uses the world and my own desires to bring me under his power.

My dear Father, I cannot stand up alone against this evil being who doesn't seem so bad much of the time. He is a clever devil. I cannot always identify what he is doing to me. He is so beautiful, so handsome, so appealing, and he offers so much fun. He lets me be selfish. He lets me not see the consequences of my actions. He lets me not see my neighbor who calls you Father. He lets me forget that all the people of this world are your children, and therefore my brothers and sisters. If only he would wear horns, and you a crown, so I would know who's who in this battle for my life.

Dear Father, our Father, when I call you my dear Father, remind me that you are also the dear Father of us all, and though you love me like an only child, you love all others with the same love. Amen.

Prayer 3

Father God, the war going on is worldwide. It's not just my life at stake, is it? It's the whole cosmos, the universe, and more. You and Satan are in fierce combat with each other, and my life is only a part of the battle ground.

Father God, how can we understand the magnitude of this war? How can we begin to fathom what's at stake? If Satan wins, there is no heaven or earth, neither love nor mercy, neither forgiveness nor new beginnings; not even a tomorrow.

Father God, don't let Satan win. Though I am not able to resist him by myself, battle him for me, with me, through me. Don't let him win me from you. Please, Lord, for my sake and the world's, keep all of us safe from him, for we are your children. Though we don't deserve it, keep each of us, everyone, as the apple of your eye. Amen.

The Fourth Petition
"Give us this day our daily bread."

What does this mean?
Answer: God gives daily bread, even without our prayer, to all people, though sinful, but we ask in this prayer that he will help us to realize this and to receive our daily bread with thanks.

Prayer 1

Lord God, I pray a big prayer now. Like Luther taught, I ask for more than a slice of bread, or even the "oven and flour bin." I ask that you bless the "broad fields and the whole land" so that all sorts of food may be available, and all sorts of other necessities will be cared for.

I ask you to give to others what you've given to me, and I ask that you provide us all with food and clothing, home and bed, family and friends, peace in our neighborhoods, and peace between the peoples of the world. This is the bread we need, Lord God, and without your help, we either starve, freeze, or die from loneliness or hatred. Feed us Lord, with your word and with the daily necessities of life. Amen.

Prayer 2

Lord God, I pray for my country and its leaders, that together we may love one another as you love us individually. I pray for the leaders of the world, that the passions that often lead to war may become passions to care for one another. I pray for my enemies, that we might all be friends with you, who give us life and call us all your children.

Heavenly Father, our enemy, the devil, works daily to take away our daily bread. He would confuse us with lies, overthrow governments, encourage violence and murder, and make us love war. "If it were in his power (and you did not restrain him), we would not have a straw in the field, a penny in the house, or even our life for one hour," as Luther teaches. Without your constant vigilance, Lord God, we would all perish in an instant.

Use this prayer to you Almighty God, as a weapon against our enemy, Satan. Know that by these words I ask for your help, and pledge you my loyalty. Help me to care as much about justice for others as I do for myself. Help me to care as much about mercy as you do. Amen.

Prayer 3

Heavenly Father, the world has so many people and so many needs, that I feel as though I sometimes have too much. I have heard about living with less, so that others may have enough, but it is hard not to go after all that I can get. I like nice things, good times, and special privileges. I like being all that I can be and getting all that I can get.

How, Lord, can I remember the "our" in this prayer I pray as a person of faith? How can I remember the "us" in this prayer, when I ask you to give "us" this day "our" daily bread? All the world seems to be out to make it on one's own, but you keep telling me to pray with plural words, other people, and not just for my own happiness.

You ask a lot, Heavenly Father, and most of the world is not about to take you literally on this. I'm not sure I can either. Father, our Father, I know I won't care about all your children until I see all others as my true blood sisters and brothers, because of you. Amen.

The Fifth Petition
"And forgive us our trespasses, as we forgive those who trespass against us."

What does this mean?
Answer: We ask in this prayer that our Father in heaven would not hold our sins against us and because of them refuse to hear our prayer. And we pray that he would give us everything by grace, for we sin every day and deserve nothing but punishment. So we on our part will heartily forgive and gladly do good to those who sin against us.

Prayer 1

Dear Father in heaven, I know that I am far from perfect. I know that I make many mistakes every day, and that other people sometimes make me very angry. Sometimes I treat other people badly, and sometimes they are mean toward me. It seems as though Satan is always pushing us toward a fight.

Lord God, I don't want to be in such conflict every day. It wears me out, and I am tempted to run away from other people, and just be by myself. Yet you say there is a better way. You say that you give forgiveness, and do not run away from me, even when it isn't easy, even when it doesn't seem to be possible.

You give forgiveness before I ask, knowing that I would not survive a moment unless you did. You forgive me every moment, out of love. Lord, when I pray this petition, remind me that you are constantly about the task of forgiving me. Remind me that you will not let go of me, no matter how badly I want to be left alone. Remind me and help me accept your gracious love through forgiveness. Amen.

Prayer 2

Heavenly Father, please do not punish me as I deserve. I know I am not worthy to ask you to love me. I know I am not good enough to be your child, but you won't let that stop you. You never have based your love for me on my goodness. You love me because you are so good.

Even as I need to hear again and again how much you love and forgive me, I know I need to do the same for others. I know I can say "I forgive you" to others in many ways—I don't always have to say the words. You simply tell us to live as though the past problems did not occur. You show us how to be friends again, without making us crawl for forgiveness. You simply do it, by forgetting the past, and living as though the bad event didn't happen.

Lord, being forgiven by you and others makes me feel good. It makes me feel as though I have a new life. It lets me live without a guilty conscience, though I do not deserve it.

Thank you for giving me the strength to believe you when you say, "You are forgiven." Thank you for giving me the strength to let my past sins die. Thank you for telling me to do this, even when I think I should hold on to a guilty conscience. Thank you for a fresh start every day, every moment. Thank you for keeping your promise to forgive even me. Amen.

The Sixth Petition
"And lead us not into temptation."

What does this mean?
Answer: God tempts no one to sin, but we ask in this prayer that God would watch over us and keep us so that the devil, the world, and our sinful self may not deceive us and draw us into false belief, despair, and other great and shameful sins.
And we pray that even though we are so tempted we may still win the final victory.

Prayer 1

Heavenly Father, sometimes love and understanding feel so far away that hope seems impossible to hold on to. I've been taught that these feelings are evidence of Satan's work on me. He would drive me into despair and unbelief. He would make me stubborn and tear me away from your presence in my life. He shoots these darts of despair into my heart, and they sting like venom at the ends of fangs.

Lord God, your enemy is my enemy, and I know he will be after me all the days of my life. Without you by my side, my faith is in peril, because I cannot stand up to him. He would like it if I drifted away from you. He would like it if I paid you little attention. Lord, do not let me fall into disbelief, either by choice or by laziness. Keep me alert and alive so I won't fall into deeper sin.

Lord, when I am able to resist his temptations, it is evidence that you are giving me the power I asked for. It is evidence that temptation doesn't always lead to a fall into sin. Please keep me from being overwhelmed by this evil one, and if I am, be there to rescue me, as you have promised. Amen.

Prayer 2

Lord, I know the difference between temptation and giving in to temptation. Young people are said to be tempted by sexual passions while older people are tempted by the things of the world. No matter how long I live, I will have to face temptations, but I don't have to face them alone, and for that I give you thanks.

Be with me Lord, whenever I am tempted to believe that my behavior doesn't matter. Be with me when my biggest fear is getting caught, instead of not being your person. Be with me, like you promised, so that my strength will be sufficient to say "no," or turn away from evil.

Even strong Christians, Lord, are tempted. In fact,

it seems as though the more faith grows, the stronger temptations become. Prepare me for the attacks of the evil one, that he will have no power over me. Let me take pleasure in seeing temptations go down to defeat, by your power. Don't let me rely on my own power, for then I will take false pride in my victory, and be setup for an even bigger temptation from Satan. May prayer be my constant companion in the time of temptation. Remind me to come to you automatically, whenever temptation comes around luring me to evil. Amen.

The Seventh Petition
"But deliver us from evil."

What does this mean?
Answer: We ask in this inclusive prayer that our heavenly Father would save us from every evil to body and soul, and at our last hour would mercifully take us from the troubles of this world to himself in heaven.

Prayer 1

Heavenly Father, sometimes I feel there is danger all around me. I get terrible thoughts in my mind that I know are not good thoughts, and I can't seem to keep focused on you. Every day I have temptations to be selfish. Even my body seems to work against me, looking for the wrong kinds of pleasure, or just being lazy. Sometimes I get thoughts of getting rich beyond imagination, thinking that will make me happy.

Lord, I know that these are all temptations that you tell me to guard against, but there is even more. Sometimes my temper gets the best of me, and sometimes I am filled with anger toward people who say they love me. It is hard for me to even think about forgiving someone who did me wrong, much less actually do it. On top of all of this, I want to be popular. I want to be liked by others, and sometimes that means not doing things your way.

Heavenly Father, these are only the beginning of my temptations, as you know, so I ask you to help me concentrate on you and your will, instead of my temptations. Be with me this day, so that my sin may be lessened, and I'll find you near as my constant and welcomed companion. Amen.

Prayer 2

Lord God, Heavenly Father, my biggest temptation is not to believe in you any longer. How can I even think of such a possibility! Yet I do. I don't do it openly, Lord, as you know. I hardly ever conclude, "I don't believe in God anymore." I just drift away from you, as though you are not there for me. I stop looking for opportunities to hear your word, and to learn more about you. Instead, I go after things that I think will bring me happiness.

Lord, if you don't help me resist this temptation to forsake you, I will certainly give in to it. I am not able to keep my faith healthy all by myself. I need you and your Holy Spirit prodding me. I need constant reminders of your love. I need to hear again and again that you bring joy to me out of sorrow.

Lord, I've been taught that my temptations are not the same thing as giving in to temptations, and for that I am grateful. My temptations are so numerous. Help me see your power at work in my life every time I am able not to give in to temptation, and when I fail, help me to believe that you are a merciful God, who loves me anyway. Amen.

Prayer 3

Heavenly Father, I need your help. When I try to fight against my enemies all by myself, I end up in a worse scrape. I need your help to battle against such powerful forces.

You have promised that you will use prayer to help me do battle against the forces of evil, so now I am praying. I ask you to take on Satan for me, and to rid him from me and my day. I ask you to blow him away, like a dandelion seed in springtime, so that his weeds cannot take root in my life. I ask you to keep putting the right kind of people in my life who will encourage me to believe, for such people are certainly your helpers for my sake.

Heavenly Father, by this prayer, hear my plea for

help, and drive the devil away from me. "He is an enemy who never stops or becomes weary" and as soon as "one attack ceases, new ones always arise." Therefore, Lord God, I take comfort in this prayer you've taught me to pray, believing that you are listening and helping, and above all, in charge of this world. Amen.

The Doxology
"For thine is the kingdom and the power and the glory forever and ever. Amen."

What does "Amen" mean?
Answer: "Amen" means Yes, it shall be so. We say Amen because we are certain that such petitions are pleasing to our Father in heaven and are heard by him. For he himself has commanded us to pray in this way and has promised to hear us.

Prayer 1

Lord God, it is hard for me to think of a kingdom from my everyday world, unless I fantasize. It is hard for me to think of power, when I have so little of it. Glory is something I know little about. Athletes seem to have some notion of these things, and famous people might know what this feels like, but Lord, I don't.

All the kingdoms I make on earth are no kingdoms at all. That's what I do so much of the time, when I hope and dream for the wrong things. All of them are mirages and mistakes, unless it's your kingdom, your power, and your glory I am asking for.

Help me desire to be a part of your kingdom, so I don't have to be about kingdom building myself. Help me sense your kingdom already in progress on earth, and in my life, so that it's not something so far away in the future that it is not real for me today. Help me give you thanks for membership in your realm. I am a member of your royal family, your royal priesthood, because you have adopted me through Holy Baptism.

What a God! What a heavenly Father! You make me your own! Amen.

Prayer 2

Amen, it is so, Lord, it is so. You are up and about in this world. You are more present than atmosphere, more refreshing than gentle rain, warmer than the summer noonday sun, and purer than a mountain stream.

Lord, you listen to me more closely than my best friend. You tell me not to doubt but that you hear every word, and you understand every thought that's too hard for me to put into words. You listen to me, Lord, to me. Only a big God could care like you, and you do.

Amen, Heavenly Father. You are the beginning and end of all things, and at this moment you are listening to me. I am your beloved child. For that reason alone, you listen. Amen, it is so. Amen.

BAPTIZED INTO CHRIST

The drawing captures the gentleness and power of being baptized into Christ, forever his child.

The sea shell reminds us of our baptism, the day of our adoption.

The crown of thorns reminds us of his suffering and death for our forgiveness and redemption.

The sea reminds us of the Sea of Galilee, where many of Christ's teachings were given. The sea also reminds us that we are baptized into his life and teachings for our own perilous and adventuresome lives in Christ.

Whatever the storm, because of baptism, we are held forever in God's arms of grace.

BAPTIZED INTO CHRIST

IV. THE SACRAMENT OF HOLY BAPTISM

1. What is Baptism?
Answer: Baptism is not water only, but it is water used together with God's Word and by his command.

Prayer 1

Lord God, what a wonderful gift you've given us in baptism. You make us all your sons and daughters. Like the water that prepared us for birth in our mother's womb, so the waters of Holy Baptism deliver us into the family of God.

Dear Father, what you do for me through Holy Baptism is a pure gift. I have nothing to do with my births! It is all your doing, your adopting, your claiming me as your very own child.

Before I could ever think of asking you to adopt me, you already did. Before I could begin to be your good person, you took me in. Before I even knew my own name, you knew it and called me your own. I cannot thank you enough, Heavenly Father, for wanting me, "warts and all," as your own.

As the years pass by, help me become exactly what you want me to become, as I follow the teachings and examples of your only begotten Son, Jesus. As I reflect his life, by my own thoughts, words, and deeds, I take pride in the day you adopted me. Amen.

Prayer 2

Lord God, to be baptized in your name by anyone at any time is to be baptized by you. It is your very own voice and word, though you use the vocal cords and hands of another. It is you adopting, and making me an inheritor of your kingdom forever.

How wonderful God, that you use everyday plain water with your marvelous Word to work your will. The world cannot grasp the magnitude of this miracle, because it looks too simple for those preferring dramatic events. You do it quietly, like real birth, and bring forth new persons named as persons of the Christ.

Lord, when you connect the water with the Word, you place all your honor and power and might in this lowly event. By virtue of your Word, the lowliest water becomes holy, for you use it for your purpose. It is so simple, that you let the adoptions continue in every land, among every people; and it is so profound, that no one can plumb the depths of its meaning.

I am alive, and I am yours, because you let the water and the Word come to me. Thank you, Lord, forever. Amen.

2. What benefits does God give in Baptism?

Answer: In Baptism God forgives sin, delivers from death and the devil, and gives everlasting salvation to all who believe what he has promised.

Prayer 1

Lord God, Heavenly Father, I know that my sin is real, for I know myself well. It's every bit as real as my own flesh. I can touch and feel and see who I am very easily, so I am convinced.

Lord God, thank you for making baptism more real than my sin. You use water that was on earth long before I arrived; water that I can see and taste and swallow. You use words that were spoken centuries before I was given earthly life; words I can hear and recall and believe as true echoes of your promises.

You delivered me from death, good Lord God, before I lived! You provided for my salvation through Jesus your Son, and you did it all without asking my permission! Thank you, Lord God, for saving me your way, the only way that works.

Forgive me when I try to add to your work by supposing that I must be good in order to be the child of the Good Shepherd. Forgive me whenever I think my behavior insures my salvation, instead of the work of Jesus, the Lord. Amen.

Prayer 2

Lord God, when I get swallowed up in my own sin, doubting that anyone loves me, much less you, remind me to quote Luther: "But I am baptized!" When it is necessary Lord, when I am really discouraged with myself, and have no hope, remind me to say to myself, again and again, like a litany: "But I am baptized. But I am baptized."

In baptism, Lord God, I became your child, and now nothing can separate us one from another. Though I do wicked things, you will not let me go. Though I walk through a valley of disgrace, and you show much displeasure with me, you will not disown me. You will haunt me and hound me all the days of my life, because I am your child. Before I repent, your arms are uplifted in a welcoming embrace. If I do not repent, you will not give up on me until I hear your word of grace: "You are my beloved child."

Grace upon grace, is what you are, and I thank you for being the only God. Amen.

3. How can water do such great things?

Answer: It is not water that does these things, but God's Word with the water and our trust in this Word. Water by itself is only water, but with the Word of God it is a life-giving water which by grace gives the new birth through the Holy Spirit.

Prayer 1

Lord Jesus Christ, doubts are often planted in my mind by the thoughts and teachings of others. Some say that I must choose to be your child; or they say I must be immersed; or they say I must "know the Lord," then I am worthy or "ready" for baptism.

Lord, thank you for being my God and adopting me through baptism before I was worthy or ready. Thank you for giving me birth and not letting me choose, for then I would certainly be trying to save myself, instead of trusting you and your cross. You keep insisting upon being the one and only Savior. You won't let us help, and you won't let the amount of water decide how effective your Word is with the water. You alone have power over death and Satan and sin. It is prideful of me to think otherwise.

Lord, thank you for making me totally dependent

upon you for my salvation, and not upon myself or my decisions. It is all your work and your grace, and I will try to give you thanks for this love all the days of my life. Amen.

Prayer 2

Lord God, teach me to cling to my baptism so tightly that my faith has something to grasp. It is the event of my lifetime, and it is so filled with your power alone, that nothing can ever lessen it. Though I forget it, it happened. Though I deny its power, you keep using its power on me. Though the world calls it magic, you make it work like grace, gently, constantly, ever there as the day of my adoption into your kingdom. You did it, and it is over. I am yours, and nothing can separate us, for you have power over all enemies, including my faithlessness.

Who can stand such grace as this? It mocks all persons who try to save themselves by faith, by works, by decisions, or by right thinking. You will not have it. You will do the saving all alone, because only you can do it. You will do it, because only you know the power of pure love.

I rest in the thought of your kindness and goodness, ever grateful that my birth into your kingdom is even a bigger surprise than my birth into this world. Amen.

> ### 4. What does baptism mean for daily living?
> Answer: It means that our sinful self, with all its evil deeds and desires, should be drowned through daily repentance; and that day after day a new self should arise to live with God in righteousness and purity forever.

Prayer 1

Lord Jesus Christ, you have shown by your life what it means to live baptism daily. As I became a child of God by baptism, you were born that way. You are the only begotten child of God; you are God in flesh, and you have shown by your life what it means to walk in baptism. Your example is for me.

Lord Jesus, you have announced the kingdom of God on earth, and have begun its reign. You have made me a citizen of the kingdom by adoption, and I am grateful.

Lord Jesus, help me grow in faith and goodness, not for the sake of my eternal salvation, which you have already settled, but out of love for you and the Heavenly Father. Every day I learn more of what you desire. Every day your way of walking with God frees me from hatred and greed, envy and foolish pride. I see those attributes in myself, Lord Jesus, and ask that you help me eliminate them for your sake, as well as my own.

I know, dear Jesus, that if the world is going to believe in your influence, your influence on me has got to be no secret. I know that if I am really going to be a believer, I need to act like one, proudly. I am so inspired by your life, I only ask for the privilege of reflecting it, with your help. Amen.

THE EMMAUS ROAD

The ink drawing captures the dynamic and timeless elements of the Emmaus Road story as seen from the village window (Luke 24).

The thorny vine symbolizes the crown he wore. On the thorny branches a ripped cocoon symbolizes the empty tomb. A living vine frames the window and the events that are happening. The setting sun over the road is a reminder that he is "the light of world." In Judaism, day begins with the setting sun. It was a new day of light and life for all the world.

Inside the room, the bread and chalice are set on a crude table, for the Emmaus disciples invited him to stay for a meal. Across the table and against the wall is a shadow of the one with them they did not know, until they later remembered how he broke the bread.

They knew him in the breaking of the bread. Even so do we.

THE EMMAUS ROAD

V. THE SACRAMENT
OF HOLY COMMUNION

1. What is Holy Communion?
Answer: Holy Communion is the body
and blood of our Lord Jesus Christ
given with bread and wine, instituted by
Christ himself for us to eat and drink.

Prayer 1

Lord Jesus Christ, it is you, isn't it, coming to me
in the meal? It is you in the flesh, in the body, filling
me with your presence and filling me with memory as
vivid as any experience I've ever had. You are really
there in the meal. You are really here with me. And
as you are with me, so you are with all others who
come to eat and drink the holy meal.

You make all those others who come my blood
brothers and sisters, because your body and blood
nourishes them, just like it nourishes me. You and the
Father are one, and you are in each of us through this
holy meal, cell of our cells, bone of our bones, making
us all siblings, one to another.

Surely, I have brothers and sisters I have never

seen because of you. I have blood sisters in foreign lands and blood brothers of all races, because your holy blood courses through our veins. You make us one in this holy meal, because you and the Father are one.

Such mystery. Such majesty. What a privilege. What a family! Amen.

Prayer 2

Lord Jesus, you told us to eat this meal, expecting your presence. You gave us this mealtime to be together as a gift. You don't make us come to your supper by law, but you offer it as grace. You tell us it is good for us to be together like this with you regularly, because the meal will give us occasion to talk, to share, to trust one another.

Lord Jesus, in this holy meal you join the Word with the flesh again, just like you did at Christmas time, but this time it is our flesh you enter. You do not despise us, mere human beings though we be. You not only want to be near us, you want to be in us. You do all this so mysteriously that no amount of explanation settles it. You enter, and nourish, and live, and become a part of us, so that we are never quite the same again.

With words and wine, words and bread, you weld us to yourself, Lord Jesus. You make mere elements into a sacrament, a coming to us from beyond us, and we are one. No longer are you apart from us, but within us, because you say so. Amen.

2. What benefits do we receive from this Sacrament?

Answer: The benefits of this sacrament are pointed out by the words, "given and shed for you for the remission of sin." These words assure us that in the sacrament we receive forgiveness of sins, life, and salvation. For where there is forgiveness of sins, there is also life and salvation.

Prayer 1

Lord Jesus, you work through this sacrament even when I don't understand it perfectly, even when I am not worthy to eat with you. You will not let my lack of knowledge impair your coming to me and others. You will not let my mood determine when you are present. You are present even when I don't feel it. You are working, even when I don't deserve it. You are always the worthy one, not me.

If it were up to me, Lord Jesus, I could never come to this meal, because I am so filled with sinfulness, yet you keep inviting me to the table. You keep saying, "Come and drink." "Come and eat." You want me with you at the table more than I want to be there. You love me more, want me more, than I do you. Though I have nothing to offer you that you don't already have, or can't get, you want me there. You simply want me. Amazing grace. Amen.

Prayer 2

Feed my soul, Lord Jesus, with your holy meal. No matter who hands the bread to me, it is your hand extended. No matter who lifts the cup to my lips, it is you. You do not let the goodness of your meal decrease even by my own disbelief. You are doing what you promised to do. You said you would do it, so you do. Nothing is dependent upon anyone else, just you. It is your meal, not ours. It is your Word that makes it work, not ours. It is your presence that is most real, for when you are present, so is forgiveness.

Forgiveness. Whenever you show up Lord, it is with forgiveness, for no one can stand in the presence of God unless you let them. I cannot talk with you, unless you take my sin away. As the unholy one, I cannot speak to the holy, unless you make me holy through forgiveness. You do this miracle, Lord Jesus, for me and all others who yearn to know you better. You do this miracle, Lord Jesus, because there is no other way to become holy, or to be yours.

Forgive me Lord, in this holy meal, as you've promised, so that I may bring you joy, and find in you that peace which the world cannot give. Amen.

3. Who is to receive it?

Answer: Fasting and other outward preparations serve a good purpose. However, that person is well prepared and worthy who believes these words, "given and shed for you for the remission of sins." But anyone who does not believe these words, or doubts them, is neither prepared nor worthy, for the words "for you" require simply a believing heart.

Prayer 1

Lord Jesus, give me faith to believe in the power of your meal, for if I do not believe it, I am no better than the deaf table from which the bread is served, or the mute cup that does not understand it holds the mystery of life. Give me faith, Lord Jesus, because I cannot make faith by myself. Give me faith, Lord Jesus, because I am no one without you. Give me faith, because I am not smart enough to know you through my mind alone. Give me faith, and when you do, give me courage to recognize that it is happening. Give me grace to give you thanks for coming to one as little as me.

How great you are, to come to the lowliest. Great women and men make friends with other great persons, but you come to me. All the world struggles to rise in society, but you struggle among the poorest of us, feeding us with a sip of wine, a piece of bread, with your Almighty Word. No other king is like you. No other mother or father is like you. No one is so great to care about the so small.

Lord Jesus Christ, help me too follow your example all the days of my life, that I despise no person, but like you, find in them the pure reflection of the Heavenly Father. Amen.

Prayer 2

Lord, make my heart a believing heart, that I might see you coming to me in this meal, as clearly as I see the bread and cup. Give me the eye of faith to see the love that was spent upon the blood-soaked cross for my sake in the cup that is lifted to my lips. Give me the ears of faith to know it is your lips alone that say "Given and shed for you," no matter who else pronounces the words. Give me the desire to be with you in these holy times frequently, that our love for one another may grow.

Lord, when I am lazy about coming to the meal, remind me of my great need. When I am indifferent, put my hand to my heart and make me ask myself, "Am I alive?" When I think I have received all there is to receive from this holy meal, let me hear your gentle laughter, saying, "There is so much more … so much more … come and eat … come and drink."

Lord God of my salvation, be my Savior and come to me. Do not let my poor spirit stop your Spirit. Come, Lord Jesus, and fill me with your life. Amen.

THE KEY OF GRACE

John 20:23 records the words of Jesus giving the disciples the power to forgive: "If you forgive the sins of any, they are forgiven; if you retain the sins of any, they are retained."

Forgiveness is a heavenly matter, even when we do it! It is a powerful treasure given to the Body of Christ, the church, to be used by each of us. Forgiveness is a living active grace from God, a key he wants us to use every day.

Our confession to God not only admits wrongdoing, but also asks for his help to do better. Sin is simply too big to handle all alone. We need help. Christ gives it happily.

THE KEY OF GRACE

VI. AN EXHORTATION TO CONFESSION
The Office of the Keys

What is the "Office of the Keys?"
Answer: It is that authority which Christ gave to his church to forgive the sins of those who repent and to declare to those who do not repent that their sins are not forgiven.

Prayer 1

Lord Jesus, you hear my confession as my closest friend, not as some stern judge about to punish. You listen closely to me in order to help me. You make my confession a joyful event, because you don't have to hear how bad I am. This you already know. You want me to come to you with my problems and weaknesses, so that you can give me guidance and strength. So, dear Lord, I come to you with more hope than shame, with more need than dread.

I voluntarily and willfully come to you, Heavenly Father, because your Son has shown me what you are like. He has told me that you will not reject me, though

I've given you plenty of cause. He has shown me that my confession is not simply a sorrowful admission of guilt, but a plea to you for help. Please, dear God, help me be like your Son. Help me be your person.

Talking with you, dear Spirit, is like talking to the wisest counselor. You make me hear my own words in a new way, and you make me search my motives. You know my every weakness, my every yearning. You keep assuring me that my yearnings for God are very good yearnings, and you thank me for trusting you with my heart. You have made confession a treasure, instead of a curse. You have made my every prayer a plea for grace. You have given me strength not only to lament my need, but also to let myself be helped by you, that I might have a happy heart and conscience.

Lord God Almighty, help me let you help me. Above all else I ask again, let me let myself be helped by you. Amen.

Prayer 2

Lord God, I come to you to confess my sins and my needs, that I might hear what you have to say about them. I come to learn. I come to listen. I come to be with you. Hear my confessions.

I confess to you, dear God, that I need your help if I am to be your person, and satisfy the longings of my heart.

I confess to you, that I want to hear what you have to say to me about my life. I ask you to help me listen quietly to what you have to say.

I confess to you that I need a heaping measure of your grace, because I am so weak.

I confess to you that I have too often made confession my work to please you, instead of your work to help me.

I confess to you that I want the healing medicine of confession. I want to learn how to run toward you with joy and expectation.

I confess that I have much to learn about confession as a wonderful, precious, and comforting time with you. Through my confession, Lord God, you are urging me to be Christian. My soul longs for you, and you keep pointing my soul to Christ. Continue to arouse my love for confession, that I might take daily delight in the presence of your Son, Jesus the Christ. Amen.

ABOUT THE AUTHOR

Richard Bansemer has served Lutheran parishes in Florida, Colorado and Virginia, and was bishop of the Virginia Synod, Evangelical Lutheran Church in America, from 1987–1999. He is the author of several books of sermons and prayers and in retirement now conducts retreats for clergy and laity on various themes regarding prayer. His most recent book is *We Believe: A Prayer Book Based on the Augsburg Confession*, published by the American Lutheran Publicity Bureau and offered as a companion volume to *O Lord, Teach Me to Pray: A Catechetical Prayer Book for Personal Use*.